GUIDEBOOK

HOW TO WRITE A BUSINESS LETTER OF INTRODUCTION

A Step-by-step guide on how to win your customers

I0390613

MARTHA BEGLEY SCHADE B.SC, MBA

TABLE OF CONTENTS

COPYRIGHT & DISCLAIMER   3

PREAMBLE   4

WHAT IS YOUR POSITIONING STATEMENT (OPTIONAL)   5

PHASE 1: PREPARATION   7

    WHAT IS YOUR PURPOSE? WHAT DO YOU HOPE TO ACCOMPLISH?   7

    WHAT IS YOUR ARGUMENT, THE INFORMATION YOU WOULD LIKE TO 7

    COMMUNICATE?   7

    WHICH ASPECTS OF YOURSELF OR YOUR BUSINESS WOULD YOU LIKE TO   7

    PRESENT?   7

    WHAT IS THE KEY SALES FEATURE OR CENTRAL SELLING POINT OF THE   7

    PRODUCT OR SERVICE?   7

    WHO IS YOUR AUDIENCE?   9

    WHAT IS YOUR AUDIENCE'S CONTEXT?   9

    WHAT IS THE CUSTOMERS PAIN?   10

    WHAT WILL YOUR APPROACH BE?   10

PHASE 2: WRITING THE DRAFT   11

    THE REFERENCE LINE   12

    SALUTATIONS   13

    THE START OF THE LETTER   14

        THE MAIN BODY TEXT   15

        TIPS AND ADVICE ON THE BODY COPY   15

        USING THE TERM "FREE"   16

        ACTION VERBS   16

        ADJECTIVES   17

        ADVERBS   17

        EXPRESSIONS   18

    THE SUMMARY   18

    FINAL SALUTATIONS   23

PHASE 3: FINALISING THE DOCUMENT   24

ABOUT THE AUTHOR   29

WE INVITE YOU TO JOIN US   30

APPENDIX 1   31

COPYRIGHT & DISCLAIMER

PREAMBLE

The aim of this eBook is to give you the skills to write that killer letter introducing your business to a potential customer.

We want you to achieve clarity about the features and benefits of the products or services you provide.

We want to show you HOW to write to a customer as well as to show you how to keep your formal letters brisk and to the point, yet arousing a customer to contact you.

For whom this book is intended

- ➤ Sales People.
- ➤ Small businesses and medium sized enterprises who work to a smaller budget.
- ➤ Less experienced businesses owners.

The flow of the book

This book is set up in three main phases with a guiding questionnaire at the end. It will bring you through the phases of;

- ➤ Step 1: Preparation
- ➤ Step 2: Writing the Draft
- ➤ Step 3: Finalizing and Send off.

WHAT IS YOUR POSITIONING STATEMENT (OPTIONAL)

Some people find that it brings a lot of clarity into the situation when you write a "Positioning Statement" for your business. Here you will have to nail what your business entails and this is why it is beneficial.

To write a positioning statement, you can use the following guides and the example that follows.

- For [TARGET USER]
- Who wants / needs [COMPELLING REASON TO BUY]
- The [PRODUCT NAME] is a [PRODUCT CATEGORY]
- That provides [KEY BENEFIT]
- Unlike [MAIN COMPETITOR]
- Whose [PRODUCT NAME] [KEY DIFFERENTIATION TO YOUR OWN PRODUCT]

For Example:

I have used this positioning statement on my own business and came up with:

For [TARGET USER] **Companies**
Who wants / needs [COMPELLING REASON TO BUY] **train employees reliably and cost effectively.**
The Product name is a [PRODUCT CATEGORY] **online training packages**
That provides [KEY BENEFIT] **cost effective, easy accessible 24/7, expertise training**
Unlike [MAIN COMPETITOR] **hired trainers, business consultants**
Whose [PRODUCT NAME] [KEY DIFFERENTIATION TO YOUR OWN PRODUCT] **lack of effectiveness resources-intensive**

BUSINESS ONLINE LEARNING provides to companies who need to train emplyees reliably and cost effectively. The ytaining packages are an online product which provides uniform training packages, easily accessible 24/7, experise training in comparison to cost intensive hired trainers or business consultants that may not offer the effectiveness and are resources–intensive.

The advantage of preparing this short positioning statement is that you will become a lot clearer of what position you will want to take in your letter introducing your business to others. The points you describe in your positioning statement will form the backbone of this letter.

The way you position yourself at the beginning of a relationship has a profound impact on where you end up.

Ron Karr

PHASE 1: PREPARATION

WHAT IS YOUR PURPOSE? WHAT DO YOU HOPE TO ACCOMPLISH?

What is the reason you are sending this letter. Why?
If all dreams were to come true, what do want you want to achieve?

WHAT IS YOUR ARGUMENT, THE INFORMATION YOU WOULD LIKE TO COMMUNICATE?

The argument must be convincing enough to awaken a desire for the reader to go and do what you would most like them to do.

Is it credible? Are your facts reliable and trustworthy? Is it easy for the reader to say yes?

WHICH ASPECTS OF YOURSELF OR YOUR BUSINESS WOULD YOU LIKE TO PRESENT?

What are the facts relating to the **Unique Selling Proposition**, that aspect of your business that makes yours unique in comparison to others?
Where are you a head above the rest?
While you are making statements about your business, have you any proof of what you are claiming? Any Awards, Certificates, Testimonials, Reviews, reports, press releases or newspaper articles?
What are very convincing are suchlike awarded or given by people with Clout, i.e. Celebrities / Authorities / Famous People.

WHAT IS THE KEY SALES FEATURE OR CENTRAL SELLING POINT OF THE PRODUCT OR SERVICE?

The key sales features are often to be found in topics relating to Quality, Time and Cost. In Quality, the risk of doing business is often included. And each of these Key features will bring a benefit to your potential customer.

Key **Quality** Features can include:

- 100% Satisfaction Guaranteed
- Attained Quality Certification to ISO9001
- Customer Satisfaction Levels
- Best Of Breed

Key **Time** Features can include:

- 100% On time deliveries
- Just-in-Time Service
- Response time to requests
- Quick Turnaround times
- Immediate service: "While-U-Wait"
- Punctuality rates

Key **Cost** Features

- No added extras. What you see is what you get
- Best price for that quality
- Highest Cost-benefit
- Value for Money
- Lowest cost
- Transparent pricing
- Payment in installments
- No Interest rates on higher purchase
- Add-ons at a minimal price

For example:

	Feature of Your Business	Benefit to Customer
1	On-Time-Deliveries	No waiting, No delays
2	Add-ons at a minimal price	Cost-effective and transparent
3	Certified to ISO9001	Reliable Quality Service or Product

1. Is there more than one person you are addressing? Have you all the names and are they correct? How reliable is your database?

2. What is your target audience for this letter?

➤ Are they in a particular age group, profession (bankers, doctors, politicians, teachers, Wmechanics, engineers, etc.) ethnic orientation, line of business, style of life (Mothers, teenage girls, adult males, pensioners)?
➤ Are they to be grouped by age? Are they all linked by some common factor?
➤ Are they geographically close or widely separated?
➤ Are there any cultural issues you need to take into account? Like using phrases that may be deemed inappropriate or worse still, may be misinterpreted as racist?

WHAT IS YOUR AUDIENCE'S CONTEXT?

What is their Context (situation, environment, frame of reference)?

➤ What is the situation with these people? For example, do they find themselves in a recession? Has there been a recent national budget?
➤ What is making headlines at the moment that would interest these people or involve these people?
➤ Have new regulations been introduced in their area or aspect of business?
➤ Have they all a common interest? Have they all a common complaint?
➤ Is there one factor that ties them all together that you can possibly refer to in your letter?

WHAT IS THE CUSTOMERS PAIN?

What is the need (what people are looking for) that you will be matching the selling point with? What is their pain?

➤ What do you provide that they need? As they say: "Where does the shoe hurt?" Where are their short-comings that your business could fill for them?
➤ Where exactly does the need arise for them to pay you to solve their problem?

> *Prospecting – find the man with the problem.*
>
> *Ben Friedman*

WHAT WILL YOUR APPROACH BE?

How does their situation differ from yours and will this have any impact on the way you write this letter?

➤ Are there formality issues to be observed here? For example, using the right terms or style of language. Consider how ineffective it would be writing to a teenager in stiff formal manner or to the CEO of a large company addressing him as "Hey Dude!"
➤ Are there Cultural issues to be observed? Are you writing into a large company where hierarchy plays an important role and have you gotten the right person and style of language to approach someone at that level? Have you chosen phrases that may be deemed inappropriate?

> *People buy for their reasons, not yours.*
> *Abbey Donnelly*

This line is similar to a business tagline: this one sentence is the one that has to make most impact.

You can be sure that about 8 out of 10 will read it, but only 2 out of 10 will read any further. The better you write it, the more chances people will read more.

Did you ever wonder why pop-idols get such a following, why videos of terrible incidents get such viewings, or cute pictures of cats "go viral"? They all do one thing: they "arouse" a reaction from people through strong feelings of sympathy shock, horror, humor etc. Your aim with the Reference line or Tagline has to be to arouse the emotions of your potential customer.

How? You move away from the world of facts and figures and you move to the world of the pain of the customer; to issues that are real and present and will receive a response.

Try a reference line like these:

1. HERE IS A METHOD THAT IS HELPING [BLANK] TO [BLANK]. For example: **Here is a possibility to win back your lost business.**

2. GET RID OF [PROBLEM] For Example: **Get off the Recession Track.**

3. NOW YOU CAN HAVE [SOMETHING DESIRABLE] [GREAT CIRCUM-STANCES] For example: **Now you can publish to a worldwide audience for free.**

4. HAVE A [SOMETHING] YOU CAN BE PROUD OF. For example: **Have 100% Satisfied Customers, Something You Can Be Proud Of.**

5. 5. NOW! [STATE A BIG BENEFIT] Example: **Now! Keep Your Great Customer Contracts By Offering 100% Reliability.**

Note: These were sourced using suggestions from http://www.copyblogger.com a great site for copywriting.

SALUTATIONS

This depends on the relationship you have with this potential customer:

It has yet to be proven that the type of salutation you use plays a very big part in getting a response; however, getting it wrong could get you started on the wrong footing.

- Dear [Customer's name]
- Dear Friend,
- No Salutation [Headline or a strong opening line is used instead]
- Dear Customer
- Dear Customer,
- Dear Valued Customer,
- Dear Reader,
- Dear [Name of Company, Customer]
- Dear [Adjective] Friend,
- Dear Friend of [Name of Organization]
- Dear Buyer,
- Dear Wholesaler,
- Dear Member,
- Dear Subscriber,
- Dear Sir,
- Dear Sir or Madam,
- Dear Fellow [Title]
- Greetings!
- Attention!
- Welcome to [....]
- Come with us [...]
- To whom it concerns,
- Hello [name or term]

Introduce yourself with a BIG BANG. This usually lists the pain of the customer and how your product or service can help.

Phrases such as the following can help in the formulation.

- Ask yourself: "Am I...."
- Can You See Yourself....?
- Do You Panic? Do You Worry About...
- Good Customers Deserve The Best. That's why we are offering you....
- If you, like me, are one of those people who don't like to compromise on the quality of anything, then....
- Imagine for a moment....
- We're so sure you'll agree...
- 50 Reasons why...
- First time ever...

- Do you want more money...?
- Mistakes that cost....
- Introducing....
- Don't you need...?
- Don't you wish....?
- Have you ever stayed awake at night, worrying...?
- Are you ready for...?
- Could you use an extra $3000 a month?
- Tired of empty promises?

Your aim is to awaken or arouse the customer through feelings of shock, empathy, fear, humor. Some of the following words can lead to these emotions when used well.

Energized	Energized	Captivating	Extraordinary
Superb	Ecstatic	Enthralling	Invincible
Gorgeous	Fabulous	Adorable	Booming
Luxurious	Unbelievably	Passionate	Sumptuous
Unstoppable	Dynamite	Compelling	Brilliant
Serene	Incredible	Interesting	Great
Outrageous	Phenomenal	Focuses	Empowered

You can also add a time limit: any language that urges action with the next few minutes is key. For example:

- Buy now!
- Get it here!
- Check it out!
- If you act now, we'll give you a free...
- Last chance to order!
- Act now!
- Don't delay! Do it today!

THE MAIN BODY TEXT

The aim here is to remove all barriers and doubts a potential customer might have. As the quote from Animal farm goes *"All words are equal, just some are more equal than others"* , your choice of phrasing here is the key to success.

Make short and clear points on:

WHO YOU ARE. Be sure and explain who you are and where you are at.
WHO YOU HELP. Explain your target market and why they are included.
WHAT YOU WANT TO HELP THEM WITH. "Sell the sizzle and not the steak" is an old phrase often used here. Convey the benefits that the prospect can count on. Don't simply list the features.

> *Well, the sales of our productsclearly demonstrate*
> *their value to business and to induviduals.*
>
> *Jim Barksdale*

TIPS AND ADVICE ON THE BODY COPY

The singularly strongest word in Sales is the word "You". With expressions like the following you are communicating that the "You" is the most important.

- ➤ You discover / You are discovering
- ➤ You have / You are having
- ➤ You find / You are finding
- ➤ You save / You are saving
- ➤ You benefit / You are benefitting

Note the use of the present tense that will convey a sense of the event already taken place and that the customer is already reaping the benefits.

Phrases such as "YOU'LL DISCOVER / YOU'LL FIND / YOU'LL SAVE / YOU WILL BENEFIT" are promises towards the future.

USING THE TERM "FREE"

Free is always attractive – but people are becoming more and more skeptical of the word. We all knowing the saying "There is no such thing as a free lunch"; somewhere along the lines, it will cost somehow to have enjoyed that free meal.

So when using the term "Free", try using "FREE BECAUSE...." because people need an explanation why it is free.

You can also consider using "FREE, SO THAT...." linking up the wanted outcome to the feature you are describing.

ACTION VERBS

The verbs must instill confidence while being persuasive.

- ➤ GROW!
- ➤ IMAGINE!
- ➤ EXTEND
- ➤ EXPAND
- ➤ VALUE
- ➤ REACH
- ➤ AVOID
- ➤ CHANGE
- ➤ OVERCOME

ADJECTIVES

- AMAZING
- REMARKABLE
- COMPREHENSIVE
- PROVEN
- ESSENTIAL
- VITAL
- EXCLUSIVE
- GENUINE
- THOROUGH
- TEMPTING

- EXPERIENCED
- DEPENDABLE
- IDEAL
- UNRIVALLED
- DISTINGUISHED
- FIRST-RATE
- HIGHEST QUALITY
- INCOMPARABLE
- TOP-OF-THE-RANGE
- RISK-FREE

ADVERBS

- IMPROVED (IMPLYING SOMETHING IS NEW WITH THE ARTICLE OR SERVICE)
- ESPECIALLY
- INSTANTLY
- QUICKLY

> *Know this about yourself: there is only one reason professionla people lose orders — they are outsold.*
>
> *Jim Holden, Power Base Selling: Secrets of an Ivy League Street Fighter*

- "IT'S A NO-BRAINER"
- DON'T DELAY, BUY TODAY!
- NOW!
- WE'RE IN BUSINESS TO HELP YOUR BUSINESS SUCCEED
- THE SOLUTION TO YOUR PROBLEMS
- YOU OWE IT TO YOURSELF
- ALL THIS AND MORE!
- AND, IF THAT'S NOT ENOUGH...
- DON'T FORGET...
- FOR INSTANCE...
- FURTHERMORE...

- HERE'S WHY...
- HOW MANY TIMES HAVE YOU SAID TO YOURSELF....?
- IN OTHER WORDS...
- IT'S THAT SIMPLE
- ON THE CONTRARY...
- SIMPLY STATED...
- THAT'S WHY
- WHAT'S MORE ...
- THE TRUTH IS...
- YET...
- OF COURSE...

THE SUMMARY

Round off your letter with A SUMMARY AT THE END. Summarize with a question that should lead to your MOST WANTED RESPONSE.

Here you have to have your CALL TO ACTION to get that most wanted response. Choose one from any of these approaches:

1. START YOUR TRIAL – Trial periods are always great. They offer the customer a chance to try out the goods without buying. This reduces barriers to buying.

2. WHILE SUPPLIES LAST / WHILE STOCKS LAST. This gives a sense of urgency to the potential customer to act now.

3. OFFER EXPIRES – By giving a date in which your offer expires, people have incentive to act today and ASAP.

4. **IN A HURRY? CALL, EMAIL, ETC.** – This gives the impression of speed while recognizing the stress of the potential customer.

5. **FOR FASTER SERVICE CALL…** – The same idea. Offer a phone number with that copy and people get the idea that this is an efficient service.

6. **SATISFACTION GUARANTEED / SATISFACTION GUARANTEED / IF YOU ARE NOT SATISFIED, NEITHER ARE WE** – People love guarantees. People love satisfaction. This is the ultimate breaker of many a barrier to sales.

7. **MONEY BACK GUARANTEE / MONEY-BACK, NO-RISK GUARANTEE** – This gives any potential customer the feeling of security and low risk to following the call to action. Sometimes it is all it takes to motivate someone to make a purchase even of an extremely high quality product or service.

8. **FULL MONEY BACK GUARANTEE** –A full money back guarantee goes one important step further and cuts out any chance of vagueness in your guarantee.

9. **MONEY BACK GUARANTEE, NO QUESTIONS ASKED / NO-QUES-TIONS-ASKED RETURN POLICY / WORRY-FREE GUARANTEE** – As with number 9, this reduces the risk for the reader to take a step closer to your business.

10. **GET IT NOW!** – This expresses a sense of urgency and a "Why wait?" approach. People often need that directive in order to do something.

11. **GET STARTED TODAY** – People have short attention spans, and they know it. If you pledge to send them something free in the mail, who is to say they'll even care or remember about you when they get it. If they can get started today, you're catching them when their interest is at an all time (and current) high.

12. **ACT QUICKLY** – Sometimes you just need to tell your reader to act. You can combine this with a time sensitive call to action.

13. **LIMITED AVAILABILITY** – The possibility of your stock going dry before your reader gets a chance to act can force the issue right now.

14. **BEST REVIEWED** – People like the idea that someone else has critiqued whatever it is that you're talking about or selling before them. It doesn't matter if the reviewer is Consumer Report or your best friend Dave; a review is a review and can be a weighing factor to move someone to act.

15. **BEST VALUE** – If you have multiple products, assume that everyone who checks

out your product line is a first time customer. By labeling something as being the "best value", you're appealing to their wallet for them.

16. TOP RATED – Another validation of the quality of whatever it is that you're promoting.

17. 1 MILLION SATISFIED CUSTOMERS - Using social proof can be very instrumental as a call to action. People don't like to take risks of any kind; seeing that you have lots of other satisfied customers who have come before you and done what you're about to do is important for some people.

18. FREE SHIPPING – No one likes to pay more than they have to. If you offer free shipping this can be enough to motivate some people. The same goes for "no tax".

19. NO STRINGS ATTACHED – Same idea. People hate add-ons and extra hidden charges, so put their mind at ease.

20. NO COMMITMENT – You may scare someone off by requiring any kind of commitment. State that there is no commitment and your potential customers will be more inclined to give you a shot.

21. REPLY TODAY – Telling your potential customer explicitly to reply today can move them to take action rather than putting you on the back-burner.

22. BUY NOW -. You can use "buy now" to motivate the customer to action "Don't delay, buy today!"

23. CALL FOR A FREE QUOTE – This combines free with useful information. It can however have limited success as people are wary of submitting themselves to a long sales chat before the quote is given..

24. COME IN FOR A FREE CONSULTATION – OUR DOORS ARE OPEN. This is a great invitation. You can be sure that you have made a good impression with your potential customer if they take up on this offer. But it does work!

25. DON'T HESITATE TO CALL – This gives the impression of yours being a helpful and supportive business. This will be viewed positively by many.

26. OFFER EXPIRES AT MIDNIGHT – Another time based call to action example. The verb "expire" is certainly strong language, as well.

27. SCHEDULE AN APPOINTMENT NOW – In the appointment business? Remind people that your lines are open and that this is something which they can do right

now.

28. **ORDER NOW AND RECEIVE A FREE GIFT** – Another incentive based example.

29. **NO CREDIT CARD REQUIRED** – Requiring a credit card makes something seem much more committal. If you're offering a trial membership for something, you'll get A LOT more sign ups if you don't require a credit card number on file.

30. **TELL US WHAT YOU THINK** – People like it when other people listen to them and want to hear their opinions.

31. **RESERVE NOW** – Whenever someone sees the word "reserve", it implies that there's a chance that when that item becomes available, there may not be enough to go around. Making a reservation is a fun and privileged process, use it when you can.

32. **COME SEE US TODAY** – This is a very friendly and open call to action example. Why not drop on by?

33. **THE ONLY WAY TO…** – Remind people of why you are special. You're the ONLY one with whatever it is that you have in your own unique way. The other use of this is that you're telling people why they are required to do something.

34. **NO CHARGE** – Another way of saying free which can often be better that using the expression "FREE".

35. **WE'RE WAITING FOR YOUR CALL** – Just like "operators are standing by", this impresses upon the reader that there will be no wait if they choose to call.

36. **WATCH THIS VIDEO NOW** – A free informational video sounds like a nice alternative and change to having to read, and it's ready for viewing right now.

37. **3 DAYS ONLY/JUST 3 MORE DAYS** – Similar to other ticking clock offers, giving a specific time frame certainly motivates people to take action sooner than later.

38. **SIGN UP WHILE YOU CAN/BEFORE IT'S TOO LATE** – A vague ticking clock is still a ticking clock. If you have a temporary offer but don't know how long that "temporary" is, this works.

39. **TRY OUR FREE (EXAMPLE)** – Have something people can use? It gives you a VERY effective call to action which you can use again and again to coax people towards your business. Freebies make for the best call to action examples, but make sure it comes across why you are offering it for free. (See above topic on using the word "Free")

40. **EARLY BIRD BONUS**

41. **IF YOU TELL JUST ONE PERSON...**

42. **INCLUDED AT NO EXTRA COST...**

43. **TRY OUR PRODUCT FOR 15 DAYS.** If you do not agree that it is the best available, money back guarantee for Return

44. **WHAT HAVE YOU GOT TO LOSE?**

45. Give **REASONS FOR DISCOUNTS OR SALES**. You can use terms such as:

    A. EVERYTHING MUST GO!

    B. EXCLUSIVE OFFER

    C. LIQUIDATION

    D. COMPARE PRICES

    E. PRICES SLASHED FOR ONE DAY ONLY

    F. SPECIAL INTRODUCTORY OFFER

    G. WE MUST MOVE OUR INVENTORY

    H. YOU MAY NEVER SEE A BARGAIN LIKE THIS AGAIN.

    I. IF YOU DONT ACT NOW, THIS LIMITED-TIME WILL EXPIRE!

    J. LIMITED SUPPLY

    K. LIMITED TIME OFFER

    L. OUR PRICE IS GUARANTEED FOR 30 DAYS (AFTER THAT WHO KNOWS WHAT WE'LL CHARGE??)

- Sincerely, / Sincerely Yours, / Yours sincerely,
- Very Sincerely,
- Cordially, / Cordially yours,
- Best Regards, / Kind Regards,
- Good Luck
- Best Wishes
- Very Truly Yours, / Yours Very Truly,
- Respectfully Yours,
- Faithfully Yours, / Yours faithfully,
- Thank You.

When you have written your draft, read it over and check for grammatical and typing errors.

Then read it out loud. This will tell you if the letter flows well.

Then get someone else to read it aloud and listen for errors or possible misinterpretations that can sneak in.

Leave your letter one night. Come back to it the next day and re-read it. How does it come across? Does it need tweaking? Does it sound real and like something you would want to read yourself?

Final Check: Give it to someone who is outside the business to read and see how they find it. I call this the Grandma Check. They will soon enough tell you if your letter reads well and understandably enough. If they are impressed, then so will your customer be!

Before sending off your letter, ensure that the customer has no difficulties in responding, i.e. consider enclosing Self-addressed envelopes.

Can you add maps with directions to your business?

Are all your contact details on the letter? Give more details of your offer – perhaps with visuals (photos, diagrams, brochures, etc.) in an attachment. Ideally all contact information should be on the main letter, in case the rest gets lost.

Consider using the back of the letter as this is often termed as free Real Estate in communicating with your customer. Add testimonials or features, pictures of awards or suchlike.

> *I like to think of sales as the ability to gracefully persuade, not manipulate, a person or persons into a win–win situation.*
>
> *Bo Bennett*

BUSINESS INTRODUCTION LETTER QUESTIONNAIRE

What is your positioning statement?

Structure of a positioning statement:

➤ For [TARGET USER]
➤ Who wants / needs [COMPELLING REASON TO BUY]
➤ The [PRODUCT NAME] is a [PRODUCT CATEGORY]
➤ That provides [KEY BENEFIT]
➤ Unlike [MAIN COMPETITOR]
➤ Whose [PRODUCT NAME] [KEY DIFFERENTIATION TO YOUR OWN PRODUCT]

Your Business:

Final Positioning Statement:

PHASE 1: Preparation

What is the purpose of this letter? What do you hope to accomplish?

What is your argument, the information you would like to communicate?

Which aspects of yourself or your business would you like to present?

What is the key sales feature or central selling point of the product or service?

Who is your audience?

What is your audience's context or situation?

What is your customer's pain?

What will your approach be?

PHASE 2: Writing the draft

What will your reference line be?

Which salutation will be most appropriate?

What is the starting line to your letter?

CONTENTS

What are the key points in your main body of the letter?

What will your call to action be?

What does the final summary paragraph look like?

Which final salutation will you use?

Any Add-ons? Directions to business; brochures; samples, etc.

Martha Begley Schade holds a B.Sc. in Physics and Maths from the National University of Galway, Ireland, and a Masters Degree in Business Administration.

Martha has over 27 years' management and consultancy experience in the Quality and Production areas in Ireland, Germany and around Europe.

She has designed and developed Global Management Systems for Purchasing, Quality, Human Resources, E-learning, Self Assessment training and provided trainings on these topics, worldwide.

Martha is an approved Auditor and Assessor for the ISO9000 standards as well as the EFQM Awards. She also has a Green Belt in Six Sigma.

In 2011, she launched http://www.business-online-learning.com, a free resource for adult learners and those who wish to upgrade their employability.

WE INVITE YOU TO JOIN US

Business Online Learning

Business Online Learning

#OnlineMartha

BusinessOfLearning

Martha Begley

Business Online Learning

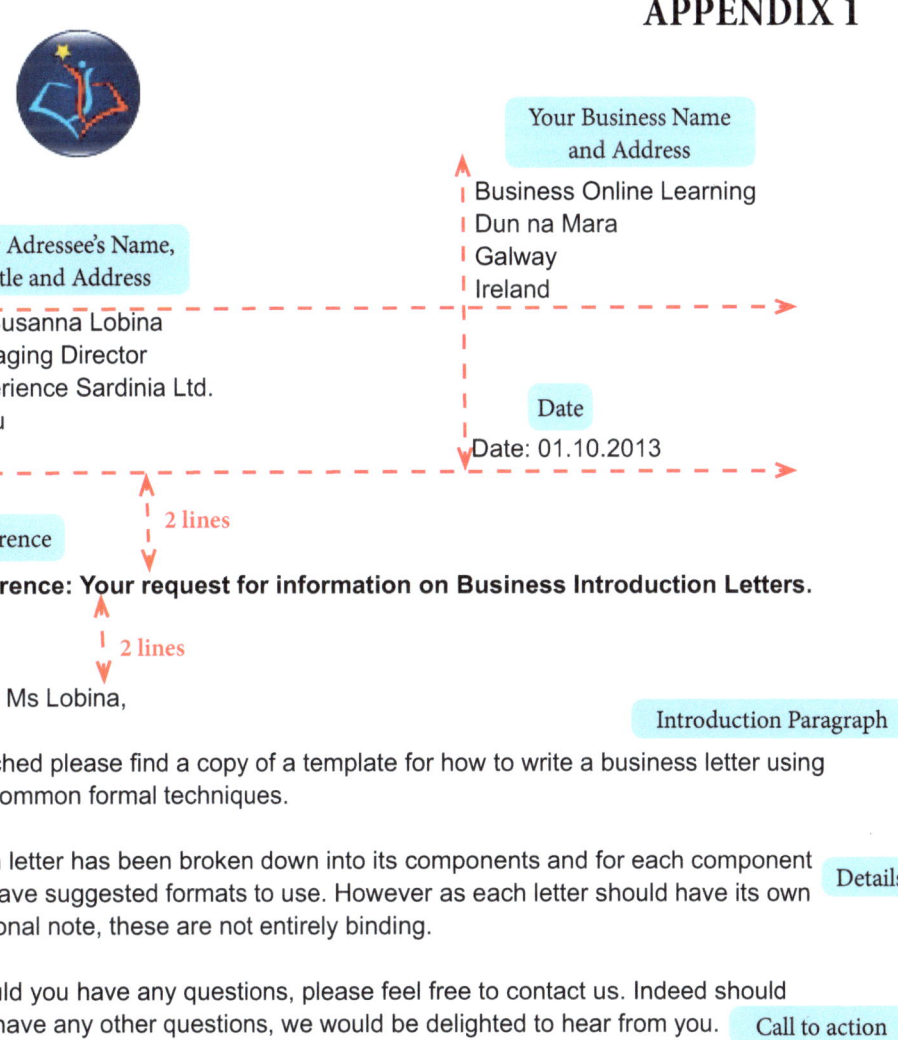

Your Business Name
and Address

Business Online Learning
Dun na Mara
Galway
Ireland

Your Adressee's Name,
Title and Address

Ms Susanna Lobina
Managing Director
Experience Sardinia Ltd.
Jerzu
Italy

Date

Date: 01.10.2013

Reference

2 lines

Reference: Your request for information on Business Introduction Letters.

2 lines

Dear Ms Lobina,

Introduction Paragraph

Attached please find a copy of a template for how to write a business letter using the common formal techniques.

Each letter has been broken down into its components and for each component we have suggested formats to use. However as each letter should have its own personal note, these are not entirely binding.

Details

Should you have any questions, please feel free to contact us. Indeed should you have any other questions, we would be delighted to hear from you.

Call to action

Thank you for your time. I look forward to hearing from you.

Kind Regards   Final salutations

Martha B Schade

Manager and Chief

2 lines

Any further contact details

Business Online Learning email: Martha@business-online-learning.com

www.ingramcontent.com/pod-product-compliance
Lightning Source LLC
Chambersburg PA
CBHW041210180526
45172CB00006B/1231